Why should I bother to keep fit?

Kate Knighton and Susan Meredith

Illustrated by Christyan Fox

Designed by Hannah Ahmed

Exercise science adviser: Dr Richard Winsley, Children's Health
and Exercise Research Centre, University of Exeter

Edited by Jane Chisholm

Additional design work by Sam Chandler
Photographic manipulation by John Russell

Additional advice about getting fit from
Dr Julie Brunton and Linda Quinn

Contents

Get off your bottom!

Our bodies are designed to move
– to run and jump and catch
and dance. But things have
changed a lot since the first
people were on the scene.

From cave to couch

Not very long ago, people used to be more active in their
everyday lives. There was often no choice but to walk to
school or work, and many jobs and household chores were
hard physical effort. New inventions have changed all this.

Although machines like cars, televisions and computers are
great, they mean we spend much less time moving, and
much more time sitting on our bottoms. Diets made up
of junk food are also making a lot of people unhealthy,
sometimes to the point of becoming very overweight, or
obese, which can damage their health.

It's fine to watch television or have
a burger sometimes, but everyone
needs exercise and a good diet to
stay healthy. It's time to make
some changes and get moving!

Excuses, excuses...

Lots of people find it hard to keep active. It can be difficult to get motivated – find the drive to want to do something. Exercise can seem like just too much hassle.

Everybody feels like this from time to time. Life can often seem full enough – with school, friends and family. And when you're growing up, it's easy to get a bit self-conscious about your body, which can put you off exercising.

But, whatever it is that holds you back, it's time to push it to one side, find something you like doing, and watch your energy levels and confidence soar. The next few pages should help to convince you of all the good things you'll get out of being fit...

What's so good about it?

Together, exercise and a good diet help
to keep your body working at its best.
They make it strong and able to do
everything it's capable of. You're
likely to feel relaxed and good
about yourself, too, ready to tackle
anything that comes your way.

Prevent diseases

Exercise strengthens your immune system,
which helps you fight off illnesses. You should find you don't
get as many colds and other infections, once you're fit.

    Keeping fit also reduces the risk of serious diseases when
you're older. These include heart disease, high blood
pressure, diabetes and even some types of cancer.

Chill out... feel energized

You'll be amazed at how much better exercise makes you
feel. It reduces stress levels so you won't worry as much.
It gets rid of feelings of aggression, especially if you're
focusing your energy into some healthy competition.

    When you use up enough energy,
you sleep better and then discover
you have even more energy the
next day. You'll also be more
alert, concentrate better,
think faster, and feel
altogether more confident.

Get sociable

Some people use exercise
as a way to hang out
with their friends
more often and
to get to know new
people too. Learning
to work with others in
a team is a useful skill to have in life, not just in sport.

But exercise doesn't have to be about being on a sports team. There are lots of other ways of getting fit and you'll find plenty of ideas on pages 12-13.

Looking good

Exercise can even make you look good,
which might keep you well motivated.
You'll develop strong, toned muscles,
as well as improving your posture and
balance. It helps to give you a clear
skin and a healthy glow too. And it's
an excellent way of staying at the right
weight, or losing weight if you need to.

Fit for life

Research has shown that if you exercise
now, while you're young, you're more
likely to keep doing it throughout your
life. This means you'll stay fit and strong
– and you should live longer too.

What counts as exercise?

You might think exercise is just traditional sport like tennis or athletics. But walking a dog, dancing and messing about in the playground all count as exercise too.

Exercise is any kind of physical activity – vigorous, moderate or light. Moderate exercise makes your heart beat faster than usual and makes you feel breathless. Vigorous activity makes your heart beat very quickly and you feel even more breathless. Both these kinds of exercise are good for getting you fit, but even light exercise is better than nothing.

To check how hard you're exercising, think 'sing, talk, gasp'. If you could easily sing a song while you're doing something, the activity is too easy.

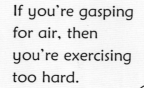

If you're gasping for air, then you're exercising too hard.

But if you can hold a short conversation, then it's just right.

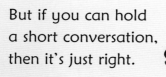

How much do I need to do?

Aim to do about an hour of exercise a day in total, on at least five days of the week. A mix of moderate and vigorous activity is best. If you're not used to exercise at all, you may want to start with half an hour a day and build up gradually.

You don't have to do the whole hour at once. For example, you could spend 10 minutes walking fast to the bus stop, 20 minutes on energetic playground games, 10 minutes walking home from the bus stop and 20 minutes rollerblading with a friend. Of course, you can always do more if you like.

There's no need to obsess about the amount you do, though. If you've trekked up a mountain or been in a swimming gala the day before, it won't harm to take it easy the next day. But, on the whole, it's best to exercise regularly, rather than going all out and exhausting yourself one day, then doing nothing for a week.

Start small

Unless you're doing enough already, start by making small and easy changes to your life that you can get on with straightaway.

You could walk for part of a journey instead of getting the bus the whole way, cycle to a friend's house instead of having a lift, walk to the shops and carry home the shopping, or put some fast music on and dance in your bedroom.

11

How do I get started?

It's important to find some kind of exercise that you really enjoy, because you'll be more likely to stick at it. With a bit of luck, you'll discover something you like so much that you might even end up doing it for the rest of your life.

The choice is yours

Have a think about the sort of things you like doing. Do you prefer team games, sports you can play with a friend, or things you can do by yourself? If you can narrow down what you like, you've got a good chance of finding the right activity for you.

You may already be bombarded by sports options at school, in which case you might not need to look any further. But if traditional school sports don't really interest you, find out what's going on in your local area instead.

Are there clubs or classes you could join? If you're not sure what's on offer, ask at your nearest sports and leisure centre or library, look in the local newspaper, or search on the internet.

Pages 12-13 will give you an idea of the huge variety of things you could do.

Before you commit

Before you decide to take up any new activity, here are some things you need to think about first.

* **Price** – sports vary a lot in how much they cost. Check the price is OK with whoever's paying before you commit to a whole course of classes or to joining a club.

* **Trial run** – if you're thinking of signing up for a class, find out if you can try out a lesson or watch one first.

* **Equipment** – is there any equipment or kit you're likely to need? If so, find out how much it costs and whether you could hire or borrow it to begin with.

* **Time and place** – does your activity take place nearby and at a convenient time of day? You're more likely to keep going if you don't have to travel far.

One step at a time

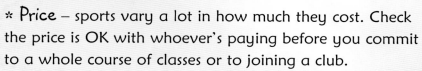

You probably won't get the hang of a new activity instantly. It takes time and practice to get skilled. So don't be put off if it feels impossible to start with. Once you've mastered it, you'll feel pretty pleased with yourself.

Sometimes, even when you've tried your hardest, you might find an activity isn't for you after all. Don't get stressed about it – just move on and give something else a go.

What if I hate sport?

So, you're really not into exercise? You're sure there's nothing for you? Just take a look at this list to see how many activities there are to choose from – and these aren't all. If you're not sure what some of them are, you can find out more on the internet.

Abseiling
Aerobics
African dancing
Aqua aerobics
Archery
Athletics
Badminton
Ballet
Baseball
Basketball
Bhangra dancing
Bollywood dancing
Bowling
Boxercise
Canoeing
Circuit training

Circus skills
Climbing
Cricket
Cross-country running
Cycling
Diving
Fencing
Flying disc
Football
Golf
Gymnastics
Hiking
Hockey
Horse riding
Hula-hooping
Ice skating

Jogging
Judo
Juggling
Karate
Kite flying
Lacrosse
Line dancing
Martial arts
Netball
Nordic walking
Orienteering
Power walking
Rollerblading
Rounders
Rowing
Rugby
Running
Sailing
Salsa
Skateboarding
Skiing
Skipping
Sledging

Snowboarding
Squash
Street dancing
Surfing
Swimming
Table tennis
Tai chi
Tai kwondo
Tap dancing
Tennis
Trampolining
Volleyball
Walking
Water polo
Water skiing
Windsurfing
Yoga

What is fitness anyway?

To have all-over body fitness, you need to be fit in three main ways – stamina, strength and suppleness. But what exactly are these and how can you achieve them?

Keep going... and going

Stamina is the ability to keep going – for more than a minute – at exercise, such as jogging, that uses the big muscles in your arms and legs and makes you breathless.

You need lots of oxygen to produce the energy for this kind of activity. It makes your heart and lungs work hard to deliver more oxygen to your muscles, so it's often called aerobic exercise, which means 'with oxygen'.

Aerobic exercise also includes dancing, swimming, brisk walking, cycling, rowing, aerobics, and anything that keeps you moving fast for at least a minute at a time.

If you do regular aerobic exercise, say for around an hour most days, it should give you a strong heart, a good pair of lungs and healthy muscles. You'll be able to do more – running for a bus, for example – with less effort. And a healthy heart means you're less likely to get heart-related diseases when you're older.

Aerobic exercise also helps you keep at a healthy weight, as it helps to burn up the calories that are in your food.

Flex your muscles

Exercise feels easier if you have muscle fitness.
This helps you keep going, gives you energy
and prevents injuries.

Your muscles can be fit in two different
ways. You can have muscle strength, which is
being able to use all your force on one action,
such as lifting a heavy box. And you can have muscle
endurance. This is the ability to keep repeating the same
action using one muscle group, such as your stomach
muscles when you do a sit-up.

This kind of exercise is known as 'anaerobic', or
'without oxygen', because your body doesn't need lots
of extra oxygen to do it.

Simple ways of helping to develop good muscles are
going on climbing frames, skateboarding, practising body
balances such as handstands, or doing leapfrog. You can
find lots more muscle-strengthening ideas on pages 34-35.

Tie yourself in knots

Being supple means you can move your joints – the places
where your bones link up – through their full range of
movement. Gymnasts and ballet dancers can perform
amazing moves because of how flexible they are.

The more you stretch, the more flexible
you'll be. Stretching lengthens and relaxes
your muscles so they become more elastic.
Besides gym and dance, yoga and martial
arts, such as judo, are good for suppleness.

What's going on inside?

The more you exercise, the fitter you'll feel and the more you'll want to do. You'll probably be happier too. But how does it all work?

Heart of things

Your heart is a big muscle and needs exercise just like any other muscle. Your heartbeat is really your heart contracting (tightening) and relaxing. With each contraction, blood is squeezed out of your heart into tubes called arteries and pumped all round your body.

Lung

Heart

Artery

When you exercise, your heart beats faster to pump more blood around your body. This gives your muscles the extra oxygen and food they need, which are carried in your blood.

When you first start getting more active, you might feel your heart pounding. But as you do more exercise, your heart gets stronger and pumps more efficiently, so it won't need to beat as fast. A strong heart can avoid heart disease and other illnesses.

Top sports people often have a low heart rate — it's because they're so fit.

Lifeblood

Regular exercise improves the circulation of your blood by making your blood vessels more elastic and even opening up new channels.

It also allows the blood to flow smoothly. If you eat lots of fatty foods and don't do enough exercise, the fat can build up in your arteries. The arteries get narrower so it's harder for blood to pass through. This can lead to heart disease or, if the artery to the brain is affected, a stroke.

Fat

Looking down an artery partly blocked by fat

Keeping fit also keeps the levels of sugar in your blood normal. This can help protect you from developing type 2 diabetes – a disease which affects blood sugar levels.

Lungfuls of air

When you breathe in, you take in oxygen from the air. It goes through your nose and mouth, down into your lungs. When you exercise, you need more oxygen, so you breathe harder to take in more.

When you first start exercising, you may get very short of breath. But the fitter you become, the less breathless you'll feel, as your stronger lungs will work more efficiently.

Muscle power

The muscles that surround your skeleton stop it from collapsing and allow you to move by pulling on your bones. They work by alternately contracting (tightening) and relaxing, and they work in pairs.

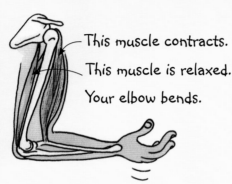

This muscle contracts.

This muscle is relaxed.

Your elbow bends.

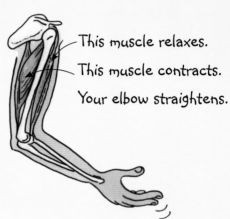

This muscle relaxes.

This muscle contracts.

Your elbow straightens.

If you don't use your muscles, they get weak and lazy. But if you exercise, they get bigger. Fibres inside them grow thicker so they can contract more strongly. This means you can do more without them aching.

The more you do, the better supported your skeleton will be and the less stress there will be on your joints. Strong muscles make you less likely to fall over too, but, if you do, they act as a cushion to protect you.

Being active helps to speed up your metabolism – the rate at which your muscles burn up the calories in your food. This can help you to stay at a healthy weight.

Bone-building

When you give your bones a bit of a jolt
– by running, jumping, dancing or skipping,
for example – they respond by growing
denser and stronger. This makes them less
likely to break. You need to get your 'bone
bank' as full as possible while you're young.
Then, when you're older, you're less likely
to develop a bone disease called osteoporosis.
People with osteoporosis break their bones easily.

Moving your joints helps to keep them strong, oiled
and cushioned. This makes them less likely to stiffen up
and give you aches and pains when you're older.

Brain matter

Exercise makes your brain produce natural feel-good
chemicals called endorphins. These make you feel
energized, relaxed and happy. In fact, scientific studies
have shown that exercise can be as effective as medicines
at treating mild depression.

Getting fit may even help you develop brand-new brain
cells – perhaps exercise will make you cleverer?

Your brain sends messages to your muscles along your
nerves, which reach the furthest
corners of your body. Exercise
means the messages get transmitted
more efficiently. This improves your
coordination and reaction speeds, and
even makes you move more gracefully.

Warm up... cool down

Before you start energetic exercise, it's best to warm up. If you suddenly launch into it and your body isn't ready, you'll feel stiff and slow. Warming up may help you to avoid getting cramp or pulling a muscle too.

What is a warm-up?

You've probably seen sports people warming up on television – jogging and stretching before a game or event. A warm-up wakes up your body and prepares it for action. It raises your heartbeat – or pulse rate – so that more blood is pumped around your body. The blood reaches your muscles and warms them, which makes them more flexible and easier to stretch. Warming up also loosens your joints.

How do I do it?

A simple way to warm up is to jog lightly on the spot for two minutes, moving your arms in smallish circles at the same time, first in one direction, and then the other.

Another way is to do a sloweddown version of whatever you're about to do. For example, if you're going to play tennis, swing your arm gently as if you're taking a shot. Then, bounce lightly from foot to foot to warm up your legs.

Layer up

To warm up faster and maybe even avoid injury, it's best to start off wearing layers of clothes that you can gradually strip off. During your cool-down you can start to put them back on again.

It's good to stretch

When you've got your pulse rate up and you feel warmer, then you can start doing some stretching. You'll find plenty of ideas for stretches over the page.

For activities where you'll be making sudden bursts of movement or changes of direction, such as badminton or football, it's especially important to stretch properly first.

Cool it

It's just as important to cool down after exercise as it is to warm up beforehand. A cool-down is very similar to a warm-up, except that instead of increasing your pulse rate ready for activity, you're gradually slowing it down to bring it back to normal. The best way to cool down is to carry on with the same activity you've been doing, but at a slower pace.

It's a good idea to stretch all the muscles you've been using too, while they're still warm — you're less likely to feel stiff and sore the next day.

Stretch yourself

Here are some simple stretches you can do as part of a warm-up, a cool-down or simply to improve your flexibility. For a warm-up, hold each stretch for about 10 seconds; for a cool-down hold for up to 25 seconds. You'll need to do any one-sided stretches on both sides in turn.

Chest

Stand with your arms behind your back and clasp your hands. Lift your hands, while keeping your arms very slightly bent and your chest and chin up.

Sides

Stand with your feet roughly shoulder-width apart. Bend to one side from your waist, reaching down your leg with one arm. Then stretch your other arm over your head to feel the stretch along your other side.

Calves

Put one leg in front of the other, with both feet pointing forwards. Bend your front knee while keeping your back heel down.

Front of thighs

Hold onto something for balance. Then lift one foot behind you and push it into your hand to feel the stretch on your thigh. Keep your knees close together.

Back of legs

Put one leg in front of the other with your feet pointing forwards. Bend your back leg and straighten your front one. Put your hands on the thigh of your bent leg and feel the stretch at the back of the straight leg.

Back/inner thighs

Sit with your legs outstretched and apart. Keeping your tummy pulled in and your back straight, not rounded, very slowly and gently reach towards each foot in turn. The more often you do this, the closer you'll get.

Can it do me any harm?

Keeping active is almost always good for you, but you still need to take care. There are a few safety issues that it's useful to know about in case they affect you or a friend.

Listen to your body

If you're unwell, especially if you have a pain or a high temperature, it's best to give exercise a miss.

If you ever feel pain during an activity, stop immediately. If you can walk, try not to stop moving completely, though, so your body can cool down gradually. If you feel dizzy or sick, you may be overdoing it, so sit down and sip some water. Ask a friend to fetch or phone an adult and tell them what has happened.

Can I exercise too much?

Some people feel under such pressure to be good at a certain sport, or are so worried about their weight, that they exercise too much. This means they feel stressed out if they miss a session, exercise when they feel unwell, and are so preoccupied that they can end up missing out on other fun things, such as seeing friends.

Over-exercising can cause serious injuries and simply wear out your body. If you think you're doing too much, or a friend is, talk to an adult you trust, who may be able to help you work out what to do about it.

What if I feel self-conscious?

You may feel you don't want to exercise in front of other people at first, especially if you are overweight. So, introduce activity into your life gradually. You could do the exercises described on pages 34-35, or try skipping (see page 32) at home. Once you get into the exercise habit, you'll feel more confident about taking part with others.

Eating healthy foods and exercising regularly are the best and only safe ways to lose weight.

Pushy people

From time to time, you might feel under pressure from parents, teachers or coaches, especially if you have a natural talent for a sport. They probably only mean to encourage and support you, but it may feel as if their expectations are too high. Playing a sport is meant to be fun, and it's OK to make mistakes – that's how you learn.

If you're ever unhappy with anything, talk to someone you trust. Perhaps there's another group that would suit you better, or maybe you'd like to change your sport.

Performance enhancers

Some sports people take performance enhancers in the hope they will make them faster and stronger. These range from food supplements (see page 46) to drugs. Performance-improving drugs are illegal and cheat other competitors who rely on talent and training. They have bad side effects too, including liver damage.

Ball games

The next few pages suggest some easy-to-follow games you can play with friends, perhaps at lunchtime or after school. All you need is a ball and some open space. Because it's fun, you won't even realize you're doing exercise!

Dodge ball

You need five or more players for dodge ball, and a soft, sponge or foam ball. (Rubber or tennis balls will hurt.)

1. Mark out a circle roughly 25 paces across. You could use bags or lunchboxes as markers, or chalk a circle if you're playing on a hard surface. Choose someone to be 'It'.
2. 'It' stands in the middle of the circle. Everyone else stands around the edge.
3. The players throw the ball into the circle, trying to hit 'It' below the knees. (If you hit above the knees, it doesn't count.) 'It' stays in the circle, trying to dodge the ball.
4. If you hit 'It', you get to be 'It' and go in the middle. If 'It' catches the ball, 'It' has to give it back. Or, you could play that if 'It' catches the ball you threw, you have to go in and be 'It'.

* As variations, you can play with two balls, or two 'Its', who have to hold hands and avoid the ball together — harder than it sounds.

Top dog

You need a basketball and hoop
and at least two players for this game.
It gives you good practice at shooting.

1. The first person to play chooses a spot to try
and shoot the ball in from. If the ball doesn't
go in, the next player chooses a spot to shoot from.
2. If the ball goes in, everyone has to copy the shot from exactly
the same spot. Anyone who gets the shot in gets a letter 'T'.
3. Everyone keeps taking it in turns to attempt shots and get
letters until someone has enough to spell 'Top dog'. You can end
the game there or carry on until everyone is 'Top dog'.

Football games

Here are two straightforward football games that will
get you running around. For both, you need one
'goal' and a goalkeeper.

* In Three-and-in, everyone tries
to score goals for themselves.
When you've got three,
you go in as keeper.

* In Pairs, everyone
splits into twos,
with each
pair trying
to score.

French cricket

This is a very simple version of cricket. It's fast paced so everyone gets the chance to be bowler, batter and fielder. You need a cricket bat or tennis racquet (which makes it easier to hit the ball), a tennis ball and some open space.

1. The batter stands in the middle of the playing area with any number of fielders standing all around.
2. One fielder starts off as bowler. They bowl underarm to the batter, trying to hit their legs below the knee. The batter tries to hit, or at least block, the ball. The batter's legs mustn't move.
3. If the batter hits the ball, the fielders try to catch or retrieve it. Once a fielder has got the ball they mustn't move, so they can either bowl to the batter from where they are, or throw the ball to another fielder to bowl. As the batter's legs mustn't move, the batter may have to twist from the waist to face the bowler, still using the bat for leg protection.
4. If the ball hits the batter's legs, or the bowler or a fielder catches it, the batter is out. Whoever gets the batter out becomes the next batter.

* If there's space for the ball to go far, you could put a marker a few metres from the batter's spot. The batter then runs up and down to score runs while the fielders are retrieving the ball. The batter has to stop running once the ball is back with the bowler.

Never too old for tag

Chasing each other around is great exercise. And you can always offer to give your younger friends or relations a game. You probably need at least six people for a really good one.

You can always play basic tag (where everyone plays for themselves and as soon as you're caught, you become the next 'It') but here are a couple of reminders of variations.

Freeze tag

If you get tagged, you have to stand still on the spot with your arms out. You can only be freed if someone runs under your arm. The last player to be caught becomes the next 'It'.

If there are more than six of you, it's best to have two 'Its' for this game.

Chain tag

If you're tagged, you have to link arms with 'It'. Together, you try to tag and collect more players for the chain. You must stay linked all the time. Only the players at each end of the chain (with a free arm) can do the tagging.

Flying discs

Playing with flying discs is a
great way to keep fit, have
fun with your friends and
improve your throwing
and catching skills. The discs are
cheap and light to carry, so a game
isn't hard to set up. And if you've not played
before, it's easy to learn. You do need some space
though – an uncrowded park or beach is probably best.

How do I throw it?

Here is the basic disc throw. Technique is more important
than force, so there's no need to throw really hard.

Stand sideways with the
shoulder of your throwing
arm forwards. Pull your
arm back, putting your
weight on your back foot.

Then, transfer your weight
to your front foot, as you
flick your wrist forward in
the direction you want the
disc to go, releasing it.

Hold the disc
with your
thumb
on top.

Catches

Sandwich
catch

Crocodile
catch

To catch with both
hands, sandwich
the flying disc
between your
palms, then pull
it in towards
your body.

For a high, one-handed
catch, snap your fingers
and thumb together, like
a crocodile's jaws.

Flying disc game

This fast-paced game will soon develop your disc skills.

* Split into two teams and mark out a goal line at each end of your
pitch. Decide how long you will play for, say 15 minutes each way.
* One person starts the game by throwing the disc into the
opposing team's half.
* Players try to move the disc up the field by throwing it to other
members of their team. The aim is to complete a throw to someone
positioned behind the opponents' goal line. Meanwhile, the
opponents try to intercept the throws.
* When you catch the disc, you are only allowed to take three
steps before you pass it on.
* If the disc is dropped or goes out of bounds, the opposing team
gets a free throw from the spot where this happened.
* At the end of the set time, the team with the most points wins.

Skip it!

Skipping is great exercise for building up your stamina and strengthening your bones. You can do it on your own or with your friends, and all you need is a skipping rope.

Not just for girls

If you thought skipping was a girl thing, think again. Speed skipping is a major part of boxers' training. Footballers and athletes also skip, and skipping ropes are standard equipment in gyms.

Know the ropes

You can buy ropes with handles, but for some serious fitness skipping you may be better off with a length of plastic-coated washing line. It will whiz round faster than a traditional rope and you can cut it to the right length. It should come up to your armpits when you stand on it. Allow enough extra for you to wind the ends round your hands for a good grip.

Solo skipping

You can either skip over the rope one foot at a time, or with both feet together. You'll probably need to do a small jump in between both-feet skips at first, as the rope goes over your head. Count how many you can do before you trip up.

When you get good, try 'doubles' – whiz the rope round twice, say, every third skip. You'll need to jump higher for this.

To get a good rhythm going, it helps to chant as you skip. See page 47 for how to find a website with skipping rhymes.

All in together

To skip with your friends, you need a longer rope and two 'enders', who turn it. You can either play that when a skipper fluffs their skip they change places with an ender, or that everyone takes it in turns to hold the rope.

Here are some skipping variations you could try.

* Take it in turns to run into the rope as it comes over, do a set number of skips and then run out again.
* Do actions while you're skipping, for example: touch the ground, turn around, stretch your arms above your head, kick your leg up, touch your foot, do a star jump.
* Have two or more people skipping in the rope together.

* Have only one ender, who spins around on the spot while everyone else jumps over the rope. When you trip up, you drop out, until only one person is left.

How can I get stronger?

The exercises on these two pages will help you build up your muscle strength. You could do a few each day, and gradually do more as you get fitter. Or you could make them part of a circuit (see pages 36-37). It's important to concentrate on your core stability while you do them.

What is core stability?

Your core is your trunk. If it's strong and stable, you'll get more benefit from exercise and perform it better too. You'll also improve your posture and be less likely to injure yourself.

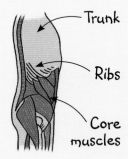

Trunk

Ribs

Core muscles

To strengthen your core, use your stomach and back muscles to help control your movements, so the effort doesn't come only from your arms and legs. When you're doing these exercises, try to keep your tummy button pulled in towards your spine. Don't forget to breathe, though.

* Press-ups, also called push-ups
Lie on your front, with your palms near your shoulders. Then push up your body until you are in this position. Get someone to check that there's a straight line from your shoulders to your feet. Slowly lower yourself down again.

If that's too hard, try a half press-up – keep your knees on the floor, while you lift your body and thighs.

* Star jumps

Stand with your feet together, arms by your sides. Jump out into a star shape. Then jump back to the start.

For variety, clap your hands above your head as you jump out.

* Stomach crunches

Lie on your back, with your hands crossed on your chest. Then, without straining your neck, pull in your stomach muscles to help you raise your shoulders. Lower slowly.

* Crab

Sit on the floor, then push yourself up into this position. Can you walk around like this?

* Squats

Stand with your feet shoulder width apart and your arms out in front of you for balance. Slowly lower yourself into a squat. Don't let your knees come any further forward than your toes, or let your bum go lower than your knees.

* Superman

From your hands and knees, stretch out one arm and the opposite leg and hold for 30 seconds. Change sides.

Round the circuit

Doing a circuit means doing lots of different activities in turn for a set time each, so that you get a good all-over workout. You can do circuits on your own, although there's more you can do with a friend.

How do I set up a circuit?

In a circuit, you have different spots, called stations, where you do your different activities. You can use bags or clothes to mark them out. You could start off by having between 6 and 10 stations and spending 30 seconds to a minute at each one. To get more exercise, you can gradually increase the number of stations or the time you spend at each one, or you can go round the circuit more than once.

Making up your own circuit means you can concentrate on doing things that you enjoy, and you can adjust it often so you don't get bored. It's best to choose a combination of exercises for stamina, strength and suppleness. Your choice will partly depend on where you're doing your circuit and how much space you have.

What kind of things can I do?

Here are some ideas to start you off, but you'll probably think up more as you go along.

* Any of the activities described on pages 34-35 – press-ups, star jumps, stomach crunches, crab, squats, Superman.
* Sprint around the stations, weaving in and out of them.

* Run on the spot. Instead of letting your feet go out behind you, bring your knees up towards your chest. It's harder!

* Dribble a ball in and out of the stations.
* Bounce a ball in and out, or on the spot.
* Hop backwards and forwards between one station and the next.
* Bounce on a space hopper. You can bounce backwards and forwards between two stations or weave in and out of them.
* Do the hula-hoop. If you find this hard, try rolling a football around your waist instead.
* Stretch a skipping rope along the ground. Jump, with feet together, backwards and forwards over the rope, working your way along its length.
* Leapfrog, if you're on a soft surface, such as grass or sand.
* Cartwheels – try to get your feet right above your head.
* Handstands – see how long you can balance. Can you walk on your hands?
* Wheelbarrows

Silly games

These games are bound to make you giggle as well as get your heart beating faster. They're great to play at parties too, if you have the space. You can find the equipment you need around the house or buy it cheaply.

Snowball fight

Split into two teams and throw paper 'snowballs' at each other for half a minute. At the end of each game, the team with fewest snowballs on their side of the line wins.

Go!

Referee

Everyone makes two snowballs from scrunched-up newspaper.

Use string to mark a no-man's-land.

3m approx

Balloon hockey

In two teams, compete to hit a balloon into your opponents' 'goal' with 'hockey sticks'. If someone kicks the balloon or bats it with their hand, the other side gets a free hit.

Roll up old newspaper and tape it together for a stick.

Horses' tails

Scarf

Sock tucked in trousers

Chase around, trying to grab one another's 'tails'. The last person left with a tail is the winner.

Topsy turvy

For this game you need some unbreakable things you can turn upside down, for example, plastic bowls or plant pots. Allow about five things per player.

Scatter half the things on one side of a dividing line, all the same way up, and the other half on the other side.

Divide into two teams, one each side of the line. At 'Go', run to the opposite side, turn over all the objects, then run back to your own side. The first team back wins.

Wet sponge relay

This is a good game for a hot day. You play in two teams. Each team needs a sponge and two buckets or bowls, positioned about 10 strides apart. One should be half full of water, the other empty.

Each player takes it in turn to soak their team's sponge in water, run to the empty bucket, squeeze the water into it, then run back to give the sponge to the next player. The first team to transfer all the water wins.

What about when it rains?

Everyone knows those dreary wet days when all you want to do is crawl under the covers. But once you've done that for a while you'll be bored, so jump out of bed and get active.

Let's dance!

Dancing is one of those things some people say they hate, or can't do, but once they start they just can't help a smile creeping across their face. And the good thing about dancing at home is that no one has to see you.

   Dancing is brilliant for all-over body fitness: it raises your heartbeat, strengthens your bones and gets you supple, if you move all the parts of your body and shake and jiggle enough. So put on your favourite tunes and throw some shapes.

On the box

Instead of slouching in front of the television or computer, you can use them to get active. Buy or borrow a DVD that teaches you dance, yoga or a fitness routine. Or try an interactive video or computer game that gets more than just your fingers moving, such as one with a dance mat or a soccer pad.

Invent your own

You can make up fun fitness activities for yourself. One idea is to set up mini-races, competing against your family or friends. For example, you could balance a small cushion or book on your head and take it in turns to see who can get around the house the quickest. Make it harder by adding challenges such as walking around a chair five times or going up the stairs.

More indoor ideas

You can always make the most of a rainy day to practise the strengthening exercises on pages 34-35. If you have enough space, you might be able to do some of the circuit exercises too.

See how many hulas you can do before your hoop falls down.

Practise your handstands against a wall.

Hop your way around the house... or bunny hop.

Eat yourself fit

Exercise alone can't get you fit – you need to eat properly too. You don't have to eat anything special for fitness, though – just an all-round healthy diet.

What's a healthy diet?

Different foods do different jobs in your body. So you have to eat a variety of foods and a balance of different types of food to be sure of getting what you need. And some foods are better for you than others.

Food as fuel

Food is the fuel that keeps you going. Energy is stored in food as calories and it gets released when it's in your body. If you eat more calories than you use up in exercise, they get converted to fat and you put on weight.

What can I eat for energy?

Foods such as bread, pasta, potatoes and rice contain starchy carbohydrates. In your body these turn into a sugar called glucose, which gives you energy. Starchy carbs release their energy bit by bit, which keeps you going for longer. Noodles, couscous, buckwheat, millet, quinoa, lentils and oats are some other examples of starchy carbs.

Your meals should include a lot of slow-release carbs, especially if you're going to be doing energetic exercise.

On your plate

See at a glance what proportion of your food should come from different food groups.

1. Bread, pasta, potatoes, rice, etc

Eat lots of slow-release, starchy carbs, for energy.

2. Fruit and vegetables

Eat at least five portions a day, fresh, frozen or canned. Fruit and veg give you essential vitamins and minerals, which do many jobs for your body, such as fighting germs. They also contain fibre, which helps protect you from diseases. (Potatoes aren't included in this group, but beans and lentils are.)

3. Milk, cheese, yogurt

Eat two or three portions a day. These foods contain calcium, which gives you strong bones and teeth, and keeps your muscles working properly.

4. Meat, fish, eggs, nuts, beans, lentils

Eat two or three portions a day. These foods provide protein, which helps you to grow, so they are specially important when you're young.

5. Foods with fat or sugar

Don't eat too many of these. Fat gives you energy and you need some of it in your diet, but too much can be dangerous and lead to heart disease. Sugar gives you energy fast but the boost doesn't last long. Both fat and sugar are fattening. Examples of foods that are mostly fat and sugar include cakes, biscuits, doughnuts and ice cream.

Ditch the junk!

Junk food is food with very little
goodness in it. It is highly processed, which
means it has been put together in a factory.
Junk is high in salt, sugar and fat, all of which can lead
to serious health problems if you eat too much of them.
It often contains lots of artificial additives too. These are
chemicals added to food to give it a certain taste, look or
texture, or to make it last longer.

Examples of junk include crisps, sweets, chocolate bars,
fizzy drinks, chicken nuggets, fries, some ready meals, and
some shop-bought burgers, pizzas, pastries, pies, cakes and
biscuits. You don't have to give up junk entirely if you like
it, but try to think of it as an occasional treat.

Make it healthier

Here are some ideas you could try to improve your diet:

* Choose a baked potato or wedges instead of chips.
* Trim the fat off meat and remove the skin from chicken.
* Avoid fried foods. Grilling and stir-frying use much less fat.
* Make healthier versions of nuggets, burgers and pizza at home.
* Eat wholemeal bread and pasta and brown rice. They contain
more fibre and vitamins and minerals than white versions.
* Make sure tinned fruit is in fruit juice, not sugary syrup.
* Try natural yogurt or low-fat crème fraîche with desserts
instead of ice cream or cream.
* Drink semi-skimmed milk instead of full-fat.
* Read food labels. Some things that appear healthy, such
as breakfast cereals, can be packed with hidden salt or sugar.

A quick boost

Sometimes you need a
snack to keep you going.
Instead of reaching for a
bag of crisps or a biscuit,
try some of these:

* a piece of fruit – bananas are really good as they're high
in energy and contain natural fruit sugars
* a fruit smoothie
* dried fruit, nuts or seeds – try cashews, walnuts, sunflower
or pumpkin seeds, raisins or dried apricots
* sticks of raw carrot, pepper or cucumber, or breadsticks,
with hummus
* a small bagel or roll with peanut butter
* crackers and cheese
* a bowl of wholegrain, low-fat, low-sugar cereal with milk

Can I eat before exercise?

It's best to eat a couple of hours before exercising – any
nearer the time and your body will still be coping with
digesting your food. This will make you feel sluggish
and you might get indigestion or cramp.

On the other hand, if it's more than three hours
since your last meal, you might be needing a
refill. Snacks such as fruit or nuts are fine to eat
half an hour before exercise, or during a break.

You'll probably be hungry after you've
exercised, so eat a small snack then
to help your muscles refuel.

Drink up!

It's important to drink enough water when you're exercising. You lose water in your sweat, so you need to replace it to avoid becoming dehydrated – short of water. Dehydration can make you feel thirsty, give you a dry mouth or a headache, even make you lightheaded, or just very tired and hot. If you have any of these signs, drink some water.

Fruit juices and drinks

Pure fruit juice is good for you because it's packed with vitamins. But it's best not to drink too much, as it contains acids that can rot your teeth. Don't be conned by fruit 'drinks' though. These are usually high in sugar and artificial chemicals and very low in real fruit. Check the labels.

What about sports foods and drinks?

Sports drinks and energy bars are designed to give athletes a quick boost. They are high in energy, often because they are high in sugar or fat. Professional athletes may use sports foods and drinks, but only because they burn huge amounts of energy in very intense activity. You won't need them if you eat properly before and after exercise.

Taking it further

Sometimes you might need a little extra encouragement to improve your skills. Here are some ways to stay inspired...

Challenge yourself

Setting yourself targets can be a good way to stay motivated and give you a sense of achievement. You could make a chart to record your progress. For example, twice a week, see how many sit-ups you can do in two minutes or how many times you can run up and down the stairs. Can you do more in the time as the weeks go by, or keep going for longer?

You could buy a pedometer to count the number of steps or miles you walk in a day, or a week, and try to beat your own record.

If you get a friend involved, it'll be more of a contest.

Surfing

The internet is full of websites to keep you interested in exercising. For links to some of the best, go to the Usborne Quicklinks Website at www.usborne.com/quicklinks and type the keyword: fitness.

The recommended websites are regularly reviewed and updated but, please note, Usborne Publishing is not responsible for the content of websites other than its own. We advise you to read the internet safety guidelines on Usborne Quicklinks before you start.

Index

This edition first published in 2015 by Usborne Publishing Ltd, Usborne House, 83-85 Saffron Hill,
London EC1N 8RT, England. www.usborne.com Copyright © 2015, 2008 Usborne Publishing Ltd.
The name Usborne and the devices ⊕ ♀ are Trade Marks of Usborne Publishing Ltd.